"DeFi is of the people, for the people, and by the people. That's by immutable design." ~The Real Crypto Brothers Shawn, Dave, and Chris

Copyright © 2021 Shawn Tracy Robinson All rights reserved.
Text and illustrations copyright 2020 Shawn Tracy Robinson the right of Shawn Tracy Robinson to be identified as the author and illustrator of this work has been Asserted by him in accordance with the Copyright, Designs and Patents Act, 1988. All rights reserved.

This edition published by Three Dogs Publishing LLC in 2021 Newport NC, 28570 All rights reserved. No part of this book may be reproduced or transmitted in any form or by any means, electronic or mechanical, including photocopying, recording, or by any information storage and retrieval without permission in writing from the publisher.

ISBN-13: 9798745762727

Forward by the Authors

Welcome to *Bitcoin Crypto, What's in your wallet?* When my brothers and I set off to write this book our plan was to simply educate readers regarding cryptocurrency and blockchain. But as we began to dive deeper into the cryptoverse our motivation began to change.

The more we learned, the more writing this book transitioned from something we wanted to do, to something we had to do. It became a calling. We are at a turning point in Human history. We are witnessing the perfect storm of emerging technologies.

This year Elon Musk's Star Link Satellites will make the internet globally available. This means that you will be able to access the internet in the Sahara Desert or on top of Mt. Everest. The smart phone, for the first time in history, will be produced for less than thirty dollars per phone. This means companies like Amazon will begin to give phones away for free because what they really want is you and your business. Over 80% of the people living in Africa do not have access to banking.

Now combine all of that with Bitcoin. The number of internet users over the next three years is expected to double. People who never had access to the internet, smart phones, or banking will now be empowered. People living in failing states will turn to Bitcoin and will be able to conduct business globally. Your prosperity will no longer be tied to the flag that is being flown above your head.

Right now, we are witnessing the largest wealth transfer in history and for the first time ever this wealth transfer is not exclusively accessible to the elite. Individuals like you and I can participate, and, in many cases, we can beat corporations and governments to the punchline.

We do not want our friends and family to be caught waiting on the sidelines. My brothers and I have had many conversations with friends and colleagues that have no idea about cryptocurrency. These are well educated men and women who just are not educated about crypto. Right now, about 3% of the world's population is using Cryptocurrency. That is the equivalent to the number of people using the internet in 1997. Over the next 3 years it is expected that 13% of the global population will be using Crypto. We are still early in the adoption of Bitcoin and Cryptocurrencies in general and we want all of you to be part of the revolution that gives power back to the people. We are extremely excited to bring this book to you as you can probably tell. With that said, welcome to *Bitcoin Crypto What's in your Wallet?*

Bitcoin Crypto, What's in Your Wallet?

1. **Brief History of Money**......................1

2. **What is a Blockchain?**....................10

3. **What is Cryptocurrency?**................26

4. **Just tell me how Cryptocurrency Can make me RICH**......................................51

5. **DeFi Craze, 2020 and Beyond!**..........81

6. **Way Forward**..................................89

7. **Can I Make a Career Out of Crypto**....96

Three Dogs Publishing LLC
Newport NC

*"May your heart
Be light and
happy,
May your smile be
big and wide,
May your pockets
always have
A Bitcoin or two
Inside."*

~Irish Blessing~

Shawn

Dave  Chris

Chapter 1
A Brief History of Money

Keys, check. Phone, check. Wallet...wait, where's the wallet!

A mini heart attack, followed by a frantic search later, you finally find your wallet.

In today's world, it's hard to imagine yourself stepping out without your wallet. You need money for just about everything – shopping, eating, entertainment, traveling, and pretty much everything else. But, have you ever stopped once to notice that money is evolving, even as we speak?

Money does not mean cold, hard cash anymore. It has gone digital. The reward for your labor at work has now become 1s and 0s on a computer database somewhere. However, this is not the first time that money has changed forms. It has done so before and will undoubtedly do so again in the future. Let's see if you recognize money through time.

Ancient man hunted for food and settled near the rivers for water. Sustenance was their primary need. But even the simplistic societies of prehistoric humans were characterized by division of labor – the men did the hunting, and the women tended to the young and carried out chores. Men provided food and protection, while women cared for the young and the old. It was this division of labor that occasioned the first instances of bartering.

Over several millennia, the barter system evolved to become more sophisticated. Across civilizations, cattle were commonly used for trade. Items like tobacco, dried fish, sugar, and even salt were used as barter chips. In fact, salt was paid to Roman soldiers in exchange for their services, and these transactions form the origin of the word "salary."

The barter system, despite its simplicity, wasn't the most efficient method of transaction. As societies became more complex in their interactions, division of labor posed a threat to barter.

As Adam Smith, the 18th-century economist, puts it in his classic, Wealth of Nations, "It is not from the benevolence of the butcher, the brewer, or the baker, that we expect our dinner, but from their regard to their own interest." But what if the butcher had no interest in buying beer or bread? Then no exchange can take place. In turn, all three become "mutually less serviceable to one another."

Smith then points out that metals solved this problem of mutual serviceability. Metal pieces could be easily stored and were more durable. However, the most striking quality of metal as a "trading chip" was that it could be divided and clubbed together to purchase items. People could then buy the quantity of items they needed instead of, say, ten times that amount for one ox's price. Oxen could not be apportioned, but metal pieces could be. While metal provided an acceptable solution for the time, new problems would eventually arise.

The trade involving metal pieces was dependent on the weight of the metal piece and its purity. Traders started manipulating the scales to get higher profits from their trades. However, weight tampering wasn't the only challenge. Another major problem was ascertaining the purity of the metals. Quality check required a rudimentary lab setup to run an assay, which was highly inconvenient, especially for small-scale trades.

These problems eventually precipitated into state-stamped money. Public stamps guaranteed the purity and weight of metals. So, traders did not have to rely on each other's honesty but on the ruling government's assurance. This was the origin of coined money, and with it, the State-owned-and-operated mints.

The earliest coin values were expressed in terms of the metal's weight. While many coins lay claim to the title of the "first" coins to come into existence, the general consensus is that the title belongs to the coins from Lydia, a region that falls in modern Turkey. In 600BC, Lydian Stater became the first minted coin. It was made from an alloy of gold and silver. The introduction of the State-minted coins made the then King Croesus of Lydia a wealthy man.

It took many years for paper money to make its appearance. The Tang Dynasty of China from 700AD is believed to have created the first paper money. It happened soon after the Chinese invented block printing. Interestingly, it was called "flying" money because, unlike coins, paper money was prone to being blown away by winds.

Although Marco Polo brought back paper money with him, the West wasn't ready for it yet. At the time, the Italian Florin flourished in Italy and had pratically become an international currency.

When the British Empire began colonizing America in the 1500s, it barred the colonies from minting their own money. In a widespread act of revolt against this oppressive measure, the colonies went on a spree to collect international currency, particularly the Spanish dollar made from silver. It was called a piece of 8, as it could be literally broken into 8 pieces for trade. The next few decades were marked by frenzied European colonization of the world. Hampered by the turmoil, paper money reached the Western world only in the 1600s.

During this period, banks started giving out paper money as a promissory note for paying gold to the bearer. Traders found exchanging these promissory notes highly convenient as compared to hauling heavy bags of coins. Paper currency had finally arrived.

The American Civil War witnessed an indiscriminate printing of paper money to fund the war. The quintessential green ink on the back of this civil war era paper money is still used in the United States today.

Before World War I, the United States currency was backed by gold. 1 ounce of gold was equivalent to 20 Dollars and 67 cents. This was the gold standard. Likewise, 1 Sterling Pound was equivalent to 1 Pound of sterling silver. Essentially, a gold-backed dollar meant that if an account holder deposited $20.67 in the bank, the bank was obliged to give them an ounce of gold.

After World War I, gold prices fluctuated violently and impeded the printing of money. So, the US moved from gold-backed currency to fiat currency on June 5th 1933. Fiat currency was not backed by any asset. So, an account holder depositing $20 in a bank would get a Federal-reserve note in return. Not gold.

Without gold prices dictating the money-printing policy, the government could print any amount of money. The plummeting purchasing power of the dollar in the 80s prompted foreign Federal banks to redeem their gold and the US government slowly ran out of gold. But this did not stop the government from printing more currency.

The effect of indiscriminate printing became apparent in 1980 when the country suffered through double-digit inflation. In contrast to this, inflation under the gold standard averaged between 0% and 1%.

By now, money had evolved from livestock to metal to paper, and it was poised for another leap in its evolution – it was time for it to turn plastic. In 1946, the first credit card was introduced in the United States. Called "Chargeit," this is the predecessor to the feature-rich credit cards of today.

By the 1980s, money had become much more agile, and it was time to go digital. It took the first step towards the digital age with the introduction of the Automated Teller Machines that we fondly call the ATMs. We had made the leap from the promissory notes to PIN numbers.

The internet transformed everything we knew, and money was no different. Amid the digital boom, money went "virtual." We can now pay modern traders or online sellers with virtual money directly from our bank accounts.

We are witnessing the dawn of the next stage in the evolution of money, cryptocurrency. Most of you may know it as Bitcoin. Well, Bitcoin is just one (although the most popular) of the many types of cryptocurrencies. In the earlier evolutions of money, currency became increasingly centralized by the State. Today, cryptocurrencies are once again decentralizing it. But, this time, it has the power of the internet to decentralize it and a blockchain network to "assay" the currency.

It took us nearly 2400 years to create money that is convenient to use and whose quality is easy to ascertain without the State's interference!

We have definitely come a long way, and what a ride it has been!

Chapter 2:
What is a Blockchain?

Blockchain is taking the world by storm. Although the technology continues to remain obscure for the average person, its tremendous applications are far and varied. One of those applications is cryptocurrencies.

Unless you've been living under a rock, you've probably heard of bitcoin, the first and most popular cryptocurrency. Bitcoin runs on blockchain. You already know that cryptocurrencies are decentralizing money again. By the power vested in it by the internet, a blockchain network "assays" that currency.

What does it mean? How does it do it? Let's find out.

A fair warning before we start – by the time you complete this chapter, you are going to fall in love with the simple genius of blockchain and the many applications it can have outside of cryptocurrency.

Surprisingly, blockchain has been around since the 1990s. In 1991, scientists Stuart Haber and W. Scott Stornetta envisioned what we know today as blockchains. The technology's application was to create a system that could timestamp digital documents so that no one could tamper with them, like a digital notary. However, after 1992, work on blockchains was buried under the annals of time.

And then in 2008 came Satoshi Nakamoto – the man, the myth, the legend. Even today, there is no consensus on the identity of Satoshi Nakamoto. In fact, nobody knows whether Satoshi was just one person, a group, or an organization.

Satoshi published the foundational concepts of a virtual currency, aka Bitcoin, that would be decentralized and managed by a network of peers. With blockchain, Satoshi Nakamoto gave the world a currency that was immune to counterfeiting, did not require a central authority, and was protected by almost impenetrable and complex algorithms.

All was made possible because of blockchain technology. So, what are these magical blockchains?

Close your eyes and imagine this.

You see a cube-shaped block that's divided into two compartments and is joined to other blocks like itself by chains on its sides. One compartment contains data, and the other holds the hash (an identifier) for the block. The chain has the hash or identifier for the previous block. These 3 components together constitute the blockchain.

Let's open the first compartment. There is data inside. The type of data inside the compartment depends on the purpose of the blockchain. A cryptocurrency blockchain would have information about the sender, receiver, and transaction amount. A real estate asset management blockchain would have details of the seller, buyer, and asset. You get the drift.

Now, let's open the second compartment. This compartment has a hash. A hash is to a block what a fingerprint is to humans. It is unique to the block. A hash comes into existence as soon as a block is created. So, if you change anything inside the block, its hash changes. When the hash changes, it is not the same block anymore.

When you add or change the information inside a block, a new block is created. This new block is connected to the previous block by the hash of the last block. This hash function is the chain that keeps the blocks connected.

Do you see a blockchain in your head now? Let us reinforce the idea.

Imagine 1 cube in your head. This is the first block in your blockchain. Let's say its hash is 123. Since this is the first block, it does not have a previous hash.

Add another block to this chain. Now, block no.2 will have two identifiers – one is the previous hash 123, and its own hash 456. We know that this block is a part of this blockchain because it has the hash 123 from block no. 1.

Add another block to the chain. Block no. 3 will again have two identifiers – one is the immediate previous hash 456 and its own new hash 789.

So, even if this blockchain has a million blocks, you can pick and find any block you want. You can trace the blocks from the imaginary blockchain you just visualized. You can go from block no. 3 to 2, to eventually reach block no. 1. Block no 1 is called the genesis block.

That is the basic structure of all blockchains.

Now that you understand the fundamentals of a blockchain, it's time you learn why this simple concept of interconnected blocks has managed to grab the entire world's attention.

Blockchain has a fascinating characteristic. Once a data block is created inside a blockchain, it's almost impossible to manipulate it. Let's go back to your mental blockchain.

Remember block no. 2? The one with the hash 456 and previous hash 123? Let's say you make a change to this block. As soon as you tamper with block no. 2, it no longer remains block no. 2; its hash changes. Its hash is not 456 anymore. So, now block no. 3 with a previous hash of 456, does not have a valid previous hash because block no. 2 does not exist anymore. It cannot trace back to the genesis block, rendering the blockchain following that block, invalid.

This is one layer of protection that you get with blockchain. But we live among smart people and even smarter computers. That makes it possible for a hacker to manipulate a block, and quickly reconfigure the hashes of all the following blocks to make the blockchain valid again. Again, it is not easy to do, but possible! Scary, right?

This is where the second layer of protection in blockchain comes in. It may be possible to set up supercomputers and tamper with the hash numbers in a fraction of a second, but blockchains are not designed to create new blocks fast. This concept is called proof-of-work. Let us explain.

Blockchain's built-in proof-of-work mechanism slows down the speed at which new blocks are created. The time to create a new block can change with the blockchain in question. In the case of bitcoin, it usually takes 10 minutes to add new blocks to the chain. For Ethereum, another cryptocurrency, the time is 14 minutes. So, even if a hacker has manipulated one block, it will take them 10-14 minutes to create a new block. Multiply 10 minutes by the total number of blocks in the blockchain; that's the time it takes to manipulate a chain. The time it takes to manipulate a chain can vary between a few hours to a couple of months.

These two layers keep the blockchain well protected, but there is one more layer of defense against any manipulation.

If you've followed news on bitcoins or blockchains on the internet, you've probably encountered the phrase "distributed ledger." Today, you are going to break through the jargon and witness the beauty of this brilliant technology. To quote Doctor Strange from Avengers: Infinity War in a different context, "It's a simple spell, but quite unbreakable."

One of blockchain's foundational pillars, decentralization, makes it drastically more secure than the current financial system, which is highly centralized. Let's consider a traditional bank by way of example. All the information about a bank's transactions is stored in a centralized bank server. If a hacker gets in, they can manipulate the data in one server and have their way with the bank's assets. But, blockchain counters this problem by decentralizing the information. It uses what is called a peer-to-peer network, and anyone can join.

When a peer joins the network, they get a full copy of the blockchain on their computer. They can keep checking their copy to ensure that things are running smoothly. When a new block is created, it is sent to all peers in the network. They verify that block, and it is added to the blockchain. And all the peers present in this network are always in consensus. With their copy, they agree and ensure that every block in the blockchain is legitimate and unadulterated. In other words, there is a ledger of transactions in the blockchain that is distributed among the peers in the network. Hence, the name 'distributed ledger.'

Even when a block is illegally manipulated on one peer's computer, it will be rejected by all the other peers and will not be added to the blockchain. So, if a person wants a manipulation to stick, they will have to manipulate every node on the blockchain's peer network. This task is next to impossible, if not impossible.

Between the hash identifiers, proof-of-work, and the distributed ledgers, blockchains have become almost unbreakable.

Blockchains are evolving as you read this. New applications are emerging to complement their evolution and add to their efficacy, security, and general wonderfulness.

With what you know, can you think of any process or system around you that can be improved using blockchain technology?

Take 2 minutes.

Let us introduce you to another concept that will help open up your mind to the possibilities of using blockchain technology. Let's talk about 'Smart Contracts'. Again, the idea of Smart Contracts has been around for more than two decades. In 1997, a multi-talented Nick Szabo came up with the concept behind smart contracts. He was a computer scientist, a scholar in law, and also a cryptographer.

Smart Contracts deliver on their names. They are contracts like we have in the real world. The only difference being that, instead of reams of papers, they are small computer programs that live inside a block in the blockchain as data.

Let's fire up your imagination again. You are scrolling through the internet and find a rare car up for sale. You have wanted it for the longest time, searched far and wide for it, and now it's sitting right in front of you, ready to be bought. The paperwork seems legitimate, and the price is just within that sweet spot. You can't pass up this deal. So, you make an offer, and the seller asks you to wire some money as a deposit. You do, and that's the last you hear from the seller. That was harsh, to say the least.

Now, let's throw Smart Contracts into the mix. Instead of bringing in the bank, setting up an escrow, or trusting any other third party, you can set up an independent Smart Contract. You transfer the money to the Smart Contract. The Smart Contract will hold all the funds you send until you receive the car. The funds will be transferred to the seller only if the vehicle reaches you in good condition. If it doesn't, the money will be sent back to your account. Since the Smart Contract is executed using a blockchain, it also inherits all the blockchain's security features.

A Smart Contract, too, cannot be tampered with and has a distributed ledger. So, once a Smart Contract has been created, there is no way to change it. So, no one can change the clauses of the Smart Contract. Also, with its distributed ledger, it cannot be changed by one node on the network. So, pretty much any transaction that requires processing, securing, and/or validating can benefit from blockchains.

With this in mind, can you think of any applications of blockchain technology?

Here are some of the use cases of blockchain technology currently being explored around the world.

Use Case 1: Banks

NASDAQ invited blockchain into the formal financial world in 2015. Linq, the proprietary platform of NASDAQ, used blockchain technology to trade shares. Banks jumped on to the next revolution in the financial industry. Security is paramount in the banking industry, and blockchain technology fits the bill. Moreover, the technology can significantly slash the costs and accelerate the pace of banking operations, making them more profitable and customer-friendly in the process.

Many prominent banks have invested in blockchain technology. Bank of America, the biggest US bank, is creating its own blockchain network to expedite the collection and storage of personal data and bank records. Circle by Goldman Sachs is setting up a crypto-trading branch at the bank and exploring the applications of blockchain. JP Morgan's Quorum is the bank's distributed ledger that uses Smart Contracts to record its transactions.

Use Case 2: Insurance

The insurance industry is plagued with many challenges like inefficient data exchange, fraudulent claims, the rising costs of operations, and slow claims processing. The data integrity and universal access offered by blockchain can help this industry tackle these problems.

With blockchain, data exchange will be instantaneous and can be executed securely, pushing up the claims ratio in the process. With no scope to manipulate data, the rate of fraudulent claims is bound to go down. As the insurance information is updated regularly and is easily accessible, the insurance inspectors can work at higher efficiency, reducing the time and cost of operations for the insurance company.

Use Case 3: Healthcare

Healthcare, a primary need of all human beings, is witnessing a blockchain revolution in the making, and it can have far-reaching ripple effects throughout our society. The technology has the potential to transform the healthcare landscape as we know it. The secure nature and interoperability of blockchains are of particular interest to this industry. The technology can make it easier and safer to exchange information on a patient's health. It can help make the financial operations more transparent and eliminate the administrative staff's burden to keep error-free records.

Use Case 4: Identity Validation

Blockchains can streamline online verifications and identity validation easily and quickly. The technology is capable of creating a central repository of people's identity. They can verify this identity with a blockchain once and then use it again to authenticate transactions for different service providers.

Blockchain technology can also be used to create a repository of documents like birth certificates. With a secure repository in place, authorized personnel can be granted secure access to the certificate.

Use Case 5: Cryptocurrencies

Blockchain has introduced seismic changes into the financial world with the creation of cryptocurrencies. Cryptocurrencies built on blockchain technology are now rivaling fiat currencies in adoption. The first-ever cryptocurrency transaction happened in 2009. Satoshi Nakamoto sent Hal Finney 10 Bitcoins. In what is now a part of cryptocurrency history, on January 11, 2009, Hal Finney tweeted, "Running bitcoin".

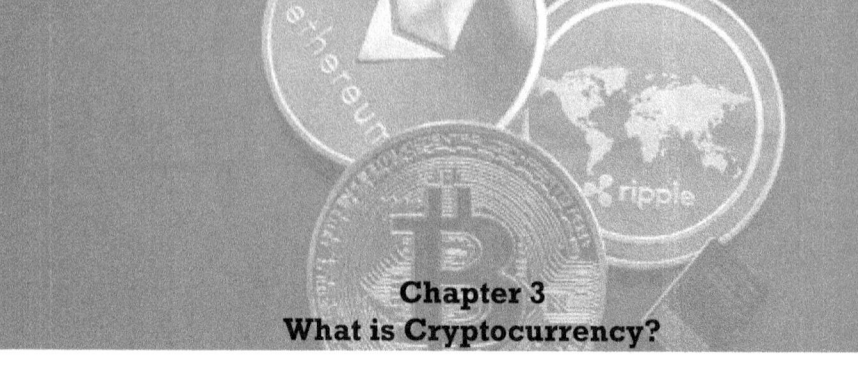

Chapter 3
What is Cryptocurrency?

Cryptocurrency is a global sensation today. Although billions of people have heard about it and millions use it, very few people actually understand it.

The first cryptocurrency came into existence on January 12, 2009. On this day, Hal Finney downloaded and ran the cryptocurrency software and subsequently received 10 BTC from Nakamoto. Their value? ZERO!

Hal Finney was the first person to download and run the Bitcoin software. In his own words, "When Satoshi announced the first release of the software, I grabbed it right away. I think I was the first person besides Satoshi to run bitcoin. I mined block 70-something, and I was the recipient of the first bitcoin transaction, when Satoshi sent ten coins to me as a test. I carried on an email conversation with Satoshi over the next few days, mostly me reporting bugs and him fixing them."

To date, no one knows for sure who Satoshi Nakamoto is, but the bitcoin grapevine believes that Hal Finney himself was Satoshi Nakomoto. He received the first BTC transaction, posted the first tweet about it, and was neighbors with a Japanese-American, Dorian Nakamoto. Sadly, Finney breathed his last in 2014 after fighting ALS. His body is currently under cryopreservation with the Alcor Life Extension Foundation.

By the way, the 10 worthless BTC that were sent to him in 2009 are worth more than half a million in 2021.

Bitcoin is highly volatile and remains largely unregulated. And, that's by design. After all, Bitcoin intends to eliminate the third-party from the equation, whether it's a broker, a central bank, or a country. People trading among peers – that's the promise of bitcoin.

In 2021, Bitcoin is being termed 'digital gold,' and rightly so. The cryptocurrency has been on a wild run since 2017. At the start of the year, it was valued just under $1000, and at its peak, it nearly touched the $20,000 mark. In 2018, it took a plunge, only to rise again through 2019 and 2020, and eventually, crossed the unprecedented $50,000 mark in 2021.

But why does Bitcoin have value?

In the traditional sense, it's hard to find the value of Bitcoin.

It is not what we call money. It is not fiat currency printed by a state-owned mint press, and the government does not decide its value. It has no physical form, whatsoever.

It does not behave like stocks. No company owns it; it has no management that controls its price; there is no underlying asset from which it derives value.

It's not a valuable metal. But, if there is a known asset class closest to a cryptocurrency, it is gold.

- Just like gold, bitcoin is limited in supply. It cannot be printed but has to be mined. The limited supply and the demand for those bitcoins from buyers constitute a dance of economics that lends bitcoin its price.

- Like gold is mined using heavy rigs by skilled professionals, so is bitcoin. Bitcoin is mined using computers with heavy processing power that solve complex algorithms for block rewards.

- Just as there are alternatives to gold, such as silver, copper, and other precious metals, Bitcoin too has many alternatives. There are so many cryptocurrencies in the market, including Ethereum, Litecoin, Bitcoin Cash, and more. We will talk more about them a little later. Despite the many variants, both Bitcoin and 24-carat gold are still the industry standards across the world.

- Like gold, you can buy or sell bitcoin in any country in the world and exchange it for fiat currency. It's not bound by geographies and has value all over the world.

What's terrific about Bitcoin is that all the above similarities to gold fall short of explaining the insane value associated with bitcoin. There's more to the 12-year-old digital currency. Can it be the many features of Bitcoin that make it so valuable?

Its Ubiquity

A currency holds value when it can be used to make transactions conveniently. To facilitate transactions, a currency must be ubiquitous. As per the data published by BitcoinMarketJournal, the largest cryptocurrency wallets globally – Blockchain.com and Coinbase – have 35 million users and 59 million wallets. With hundreds of more wallet services available on the internet, it is safe to assume that the total number is considerably high. It is also interesting to note that the number of daily Bitcoin transactions has steadily increased and nearly touched the 1 million mark in 2020.

With millions of people accepting Bitcoin as a valid tender for making purchases, more people have started using it as a currency. The ubiquity of bitcoin makes it a store of value.

It's Anonymity

Bitcoin does not record the identities of the parties involved in its chain. But every transaction performed on the blockchain is visible across the distributed ledger. So, although these transactions are anonymous, they are not private.

The anonymity offered by Bitcoin has been one of the many reasons for its popularity. As the currency becomes more ubiquitous it draws increasing scrutiny from the world's governments. Their financial systems are interested in the Bitcoin wallets, their details, and how to bring them under the scanner. Bitcoin transactions are reasonably anonymous, making them attractive to people looking to either safeguard their transactions from prying eyes or evade the System.

It's Limited in Supply

There are a total of 21 million Bitcoins. That's the maximum number of bitcoins that can ever be mined. That's the outer limit within which millions of Bitcoin transactions are taking place every day. So, Bitcoin may also derive its value from the simple rule of demand and supply.

It's Security

The security accorded by Bitcoin is also a source of its value. Given the robust security infrastructure offered by blockchain technology, Bitcoin provides more protection than any centralized finance system out there. That is the precise reason why more and more people are joining the Bitcoin bandwagon and finding it safe to carry out their daily transactions.

Its Value

For those with a rigid idea of money, it is quite challenging to understand the inherent value of Bitcoin. After all, how can money be created out of thin air?

A paper published by Daniel Krawisz in 2013 titled "The Original Value of Bitcoins" explains the curious case of Bitcoins beautifully. He says,

"I believe that this reaction has to do with misattribution of the reasons that fiat currencies (and bitcoins by analogy) are unsustainable, as compared with the reasons that gold is superior. Gold has obvious productive uses; dollars and bitcoins do not. However, gold is not stable, and the dollar unstable for those reasons. Rather, the dollar is unstable because the organization issuing it is presently tampering with it. If the tampering should stop and the government should provide real evidence that it will manage the dollar responsibly, then there will be no reason to expect the dollar to be unstable after that.

On the other hand, because gold has obvious and widespread productive uses, its price cannot go to zero as long as it still has these uses. The same argument cannot be made of bitcoins, but it does not follow that bitcoins' value will go to zero or is likely to go to zero: once again, the best argument is provided by Šurda, who asks, "If Bitcoin fails, what would replace it?" As long as Bitcoin has uses which are impossible with any other currency and as long as it remains competitive against other currencies and payment systems, it will not entirely collapse in value."

Bitcoin's source of value becomes easier to understand once you abandon the superficial idea of money and get a grip on the concept of money as it was at the beginning of the 20th century. This is long before even a rudimentary idea of blockchain or bitcoins existed.

In 1912, Ludwig von Mises published a historical paper that introduced the world to the origins and value of money. Titled "The Theory of Money and Credit" and printed in German, it was an instant hit in Europe. It was soon translated into English. The paper discussed where money came from and traced the origins of its derived value. It answered a fundamental question of what determines the price of money in terms of products and services.

Before Mises, the value of money was attributed to the ease it brought to transactions. But Mises stated that the only way money could have any value is by tracing back its value in time as a bartered commodity. As he puts it,

"The theory of the value of money as such can trace back the objective exchange value of money only to that point where it ceases to be the value of money and becomes merely the value of a commodity.... If in this way we continually go farther and farther back, we must eventually arrive at a point where we no longer find any component in the objective exchange value of money that arises from valuations based on the function of money as a common medium of exchange; where the value of money is nothing other than the value of an object that is useful in some other way than as money.... Before it was usual to acquire goods in the market, not for personal consumption, but simply in order to exchange them again for the goods that were really wanted, each individual commodity was only accredited with that value given by the subjective valuations based on its direct utility."

So, the salt paid to Roman soldiers would not have any value had it not been useful for cooking and preservation. So, superficially, according to Mises' theory, Bitcoin should have zero value as money. Bitcoin cannot be eaten, it cannot keep you warm, and it cannot be molded into jewelry, although it can do many other things. Bitcoin only allows indirect exchange for products and services. And yet, it is used as money today.

The many retail outlets accepting bitcoins and the thriving bitcoin exchanges will attest to that. So, does the applicability of the highly celebrated Mises' theory end with digital currency?

No, it does not. We are just interpreting it with a very narrow lens.

We started with the history of money because it is crucial to understand how money derives its value. The regression theorem put out by Mises helps you connect the dots from pre-historic money to Bitcoin. Bitcoin did not always have value, but it always had a use. It was a unit of accounting that was connected to a ledger. The ledger is the source of its value.

People usually try to find value in Bitcoin, but it is not the currency that holds value; it is the payment system backing it. Bitcoin is only a numerical value that you are placing on the blockchain technology behind it. This idea is not immediately apparent because never before has a unit of money and its payment system been so closely intertwined.

Even in his white paper, Satoshi Nakamoto talks about the payment system's primary role in his proposed system of money.

"A purely peer-to-peer version of electronic cash would allow online payments to be sent directly from one party to another without going through a financial institution... We propose a solution to the double-spending problem using a peer-to-peer network. The network timestamps transactions by hashing them into an ongoing chain of hash-based proof-of-work, forming a record that cannot be changed without redoing the proof-of-work."

In the words of the inventor of Bitcoin, the innovation is not Bitcoin itself but the payment system supporting it. The coin is a reflection of the value of the payment network. Once it was out in the market, it took 10 months to be assigned any value.

When you think of bitcoin, don't perceive its value as a standalone currency, it should always be seen in conjunction with the innovative payment system attached with it.

Moreover, bitcoin was not valued out of thin air. It was in the market for months, getting tested and fixed before it could command any value. People used Bitcoin; they found it useful because of the convenient, fungible, divisible, durable, and (now) scarce nature of the coin.

On October 5, 2009, $1 was equal to 1309.3 bitcoins. At the time, it was considered overpriced! Go figure. Had you spent $100 to purchase bitcoins then, you could sell them and become a billionaire in 2021.

More Cyptocurrencies

For most people, bitcoin has become synonymous with cryptocurrency. However, the truth is that bitcoin is merely a type of cryptocurrency. Every bitcoin is a cryptocurrency, but not every cryptocurrency is a bitcoin.

A cryptocurrency is an entirely decentralized and fully encrypted digital currency that supports digital transactions. Unlike cash, it does not exist in any physical form. You can use cryptocurrency in lieu of money to buy goods and services. However, the most noise is made by the people who invest in cryptocurrency as a financial asset. Given the deregulated nature of cryptocurrency, it is a risky investment. Its value has seen abysmal lows and astronomical highs over short periods.

After Bitcoin came into existence and proved blockchain's utility as a payment system, many other cryptocurrencies have found their way into the market. In fact, a new cryptocurrency is added to the list almost every day. A few notable names are Ethereum, Litecoin, Ripple, Monero, Peercoin, Nxt, and Dash, among others. All these cryptocurrencies, besides bitcoin, are collectively called altcoins. An altcoin is any cryptocurrency other than Bitcoin.

However, a growing section of experts believes that Ethereum cannot be considered an altcoin. They argue that for a cryptocurrency to qualify as an AltCoin, it should primarily be a store of value like Bitcoin. However, Ethereum does not fulfill this criterion. Let's see how Ethereum is different from Bitcoin.

Ethereum is arguably the second most popular cryptocurrency on the market. It certainly is second to Bitcoin in market capitalization. Fundamentally, both Bitcoin and Ethereum are similar. They run on blockchain technology. But, once you start digging deeper, the differences begin to show.

At origin, Bitcoin did not raise any funds. Miners had to mine the network to earn Bitcoins. The inventor, Satoshi Nakamoto, himself mined around 1 million BTC. From what's known, Satoshi has never spent any of his original bitcoins. He just vanished off the face of the internet around 2011.

Ethereum's origin story is not shrouded in mystery like Bitcoin. It came into being in 2013 with the white paper published by Vitalik Buterin. Following the paper's publishing, an ICO was held in 2014, where pre-mined Ethereum was distributed among the investors. An ICO is an initial coin offering that works exactly like an IPO in the stock markets. Buterin is still very much a part of the Ethereum project.

The primary difference between the two cryptocurrencies is the purpose for which they were created. Bitcoin was created to offer an alternative to the existing financial system. Bitcoin is a transfer and store of value. The data size of each transaction determines the fee of the transaction.

On the other hand, Ethereum exists to facilitate and monetize the use of Ethereum smart contracts and the decentralized app platform. The native coin of the Ethereum network is called Ether. Think of the Ethereum network as a service; you pay the network to run your code on the network. It does not aim to be a decentralized global currency, but a decentralized supercomputer with nodes worldwide. The current notable use cases of Ethereum include Decentralized Finance or DeFi and gaming. However, it is used as a digital currency by many people, although it is not Ether's intended purpose.

The two cryptocurrencies also differ in scripting languages. Bitcoin uses the simple script language that keeps the system robust and immune to bugs that may plague more complex languages. It also means that Bitcoin usually supports simple smart contracts. It is possible to run more complex contracts on bitcoin, but that is too technical to get into right now. The bitcoin community does not mind it because bitcoin's primary focus is offering resistance to censorship, centralization, and regulation of transactions.

Ethereum, as we said, is a smart contracts platform, and therefore, requires more complex logic to run. Naturally, it is also plagued by more bugs, which have hurt the platform badly in the past. Interestingly, although people have lost millions of dollars in Ether because of these bugs, the Ether community does not mind such sporadic events when compared to the benefits of the Ethereum platform. Of course, the network administrators are continually working on weeding out such bugs and minimizing such risks.

The monetary policy of both the coins is diagonally opposite too. The Bitcoin protocol counters the inflation rate in Bitcoins by keeping the coins in limited supply. So, there will never be more than 21 million bitcoins in circulation. There are only 2-3 million bitcoins left to be mined now. Each block of bitcoin in 2020 produced 6.25 bitcoins, and it takes around 10 minutes per block. Every 4 years, the rate of emission of bitcoins halves.

Ethereum has no upper limit for the number of Ether coins in circulation in the network. So, in theory, it's infinite. The emission rate for Ether is 2 per block, and Ethereum produces a block every 15 seconds, so 480 Ether per hour. Changes are coming to Ethereum. Ether 2.0 will make Ether a deflationary asset. Essentially for every transaction taking place on Ethereum a set amount of Ethereum will be burned. Ultimately the rate of Ethereum being burned will be larger than the amount of Ethereum being produced.

For a wider adoption by the financial industry and the masses, cryptocurrencies must support high-volume transactions. The higher the number of transactions a network supports, the more quickly it will be adopted by various stakeholders. In the case of the Bitcoin network, 4 transactions can take place every second. For Ethereum, the number is 15 transactions per second. This is made possible by the decentralized proof of work network design of the two cryptocurrencies. However, with a second-layer Lightning Network, bitcoin can increase the speed of its transactions to millions per second. For Ethereum, solutions like Raiden and Proof of Stake increase the network throughput.

If you go into more technical details, you will find more and more differences between the intent, operations, maintenance, and use cases of both the Bitcoin and the Ethereum network.

Now that you have a better idea about the king of cryptocurrency, Bitcoin, and "not an altcoin" Ether, let's move on to the other popular altcoins. We'll keep these introductions brief. Let's tell you what the cryptocurrency creators say about their own creations.

Litecoin

According to the official website, "Litecoin is a peer-to-peer Internet currency that enables instant, near-zero cost payments to anyone in the world. Litecoin is an open source, global payment network that is fully decentralized without any central authorities."

Dash

The mission statement for the cryptocurrency reads, "Dash (DASH) is an open sourced, privacy-centric digital currency with instant transactions. It allows you to keep your finances private as you make transactions without waits, similar to cash."

Maker

MakerDAO has designed the Maker token. MakerDAO has two coins – Maker and DAI. DAI is a stablecoin, which means it was created to provide stability to highly volatile cryptocurrencies. Maker provides stability to DAI. Traditional stablecoins are pegged against assets in the real world like fiat currencies to keep them at a stable price. However, to counter the problems with this system, Maker is used as a stablecoin for DAI. Maker is created and destroyed to keep DAI stable and at a value equivalent to $1. It runs on the Ethereum platform.

Compound

Another decentralized financial protocol, Compound, also runs on the Ethereum network. The goal of the Compound platform is to create an ecosystem of lenders and borrowers. The lenders can use their digital currency while the borrowers can get secure and easy access to loans without involving third-party regulators. The transparency and the security of the platform are made possible by virtue of smart contracts.

Tron

TRON is a digital currency developed for the entertainment industry. Founded in Singapore, the TRON platform was built to offer a decentralized platform to content creators. The idea was to cut down the middlemen like Apple Play Store and allow the content creators to get funds directly from their paying customers. Since its launch, it has expanded beyond the entertainment industry.

Aave

A leading decentralized finance platform, Aave is built on the Ethereum blockchain. The Aave platform allows its users to lend and borrow a whole range of digital currencies. It charges fees and offers rewards while making these transactions. Lenders deposit funds into a currency of their choice and receive rewards. Borrowers can then access their funds. Borrowers pay interest for easy access to funds.

Ripple

It is both a cryptocurrency and a payment system that works as a remittance network and a currency exchange. Built on the open-source protocol, Ripple supports multiple types of tokens representing cryptocurrency, fiat currency, commodities, mobile minutes, or any other unit with a perceived value. Ripple connects retail and institutional clients to transact money and many other commodities via its network.

Nxt

Nxt uses blockchain technology to create an independent ecosystem of decentralized features, which require Nxt currency to function. Most altcoins modify the original Bitcoin code to create new currencies, but not Nxt. Their developers wrote their own code from scratch, intending to improve upon and expand the application of blockchain technology. Their areas of focus include secure cloud storage, application development, and other similar services.

Now that you have a firm grasp of the basics of blockchain technology and cryptocurrency, the time is finally here. Let us tell you how cryptocurrency can make you rich!

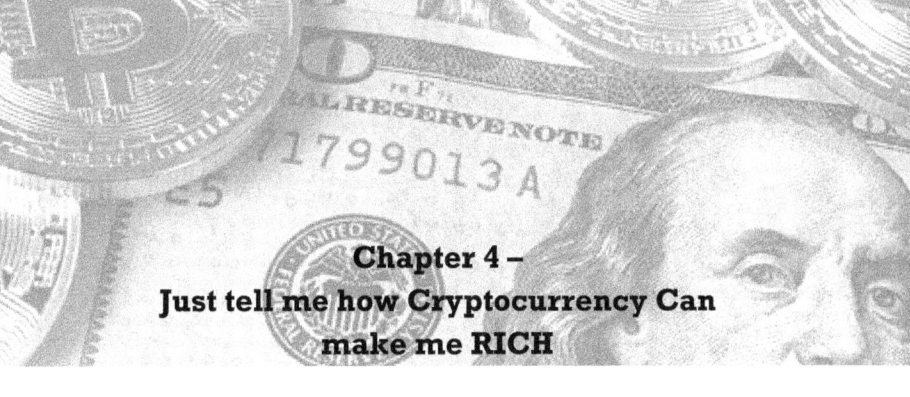

Chapter 4 –
Just tell me how Cryptocurrency Can make me RICH

If you have jumped directly to this topic, welcome! We understand that this is the good stuff you want to know, but we highly recommend you take the rite of passage. You will be much more informed and better placed to take advantage of all the strategies we share with you here.

With the stories of overnight millionaires becoming order of the day after 2017, it is natural to jump into the cryptocurrency money maker. But, more often than not, investors lose their money when they just blindly follow trends instead of putting in due research behind their investment.

In a high-paced and developing space like cryptocurrency, it is better to learn what not to do before you firm up your investment strategy.

So, are you ready for a crash course on how NOT to invest in cryptocurrency? Let's do it!

Bad Strategy#1: Buying HIGH and Selling LOW

Prima facie, it is obvious that you should not do this. If you want to earn money, you must buy low and sell high. However, the strategy is not as obvious when you are in the heat of the crypto exchange. You see a cryptocurrency making a bull run and you dive deep into it, only for it to crash and burn along with your cash.

Let's give you one example. You are looking at a price chart for Bitcoin in December, 2017. Bitcoin is flirting with the $20,000 levels and you hear a lot of positive chatter about how "it's going to double in a few months." You find your savings account and empty it into your Bitcoin wallet; then the market corrects. It shaves off billions of dollars from the market and you panic. You want to cut your losses, and you pull out of the market at the $11,000 mark. A few days pass and you find the market again corrected itself to $16,000. In hindsight, if you had held that investment in Bitcoin, it would have indeed more than doubled in 2021. You think you made the best decision with the information available at that moment, but did you? You bought high and sold low. Now, do you understand the kind of uncertainty that leads you to follow an obviously bad strategy?

Let us tell you how you can overcome that feeling of missing out and battle that surge of panic in order to make a more informed decision.

You can counter this bad strategy with the good strategy of cost averaging. We will keep the math simple.

Let's say you have $300 to invest.

Seeing the upward trajectory, you invested all the money when the price of a Bitcoin was $200, and you get 1.5 coins and the price falls.

Instead, start investing once a week keeping track of the price of Bitcoin.

Week 1: You put in the first $100 when the market was at a high of $200, so you now have 0.5 BTC.

Week 2: Before you buy again, the price takes a 50% plunge and is now $100 per BTC. It is time to invest your next $100. You get 1 BTC. Now, your first investment may have dropped 50% in value, but you have nullified that loss by buying 1 coin at 50% less cost. You now have 1.5 BTC in total. The same amount of BTC you would have had if you invested your entire $300 at $200 dollars per coin, and you still have $100 dollars to invest.

Week 3: Bitcoin leaps up, this time jumping to $300. You now deploy your last $100 and get 0.3 BTC. So, in total, you were able to buy 1.8 BTC even when the market fluctuated.

With the one-time investment, your $300 grew to become $450. But, with your staggered investment, the same $300 grew to $540. That's nearly $100 more earned on the same $300 initial investment. Point three BTC might not seem like a big difference, but at the time of this writing, the difference between 1 BTC and 1.3 BTC is $16,000! Many forecasts project BTC to be over $100,000 by the end of 2021. That means a .3 BTC difference would be enough to buy a car.

This strategy prevents you from panic selling and is a good way to stop yourself from investing more than you can afford to lose. More on that later.

Bad Strategy#2: Investing in Cheap Coins Because That's How Bitcoin Started

When you invest in cheap coins with the dream of becoming a billionaire with your $1000 initial investment, that's not really a great strategy. At this point, you are only looking at one unit of the coin and not taking a holistic view. Allow us to explain.

For your coin to grow you need it to create a buzz in the market, have multiple use cases, a reputed promoter, and so on. If you are putting your money in cryptocurrency because it's the new investment fad in town, you are going to go down. If you are buying a cryptocurrency because your friend heard a colleague talking to the boss about a new coin on the block then think again. Altcoins can give good profits, but beginners usually lose money on them. The reason being that new investors freak out as the cryptocurrency starts to go down and they sell (see Bad Strategy #1). The only way not to panic is to do your own research. Do you really believe in this hypothetical new alt coin? How is the new alt coin intended to be used? Can you describe how it has value? What sources of information are you relying on?

Most cryptocurrencies crash and burn. It is more likely the new cryptocurrency and your investment will fall to zero. It goes without saying, there's an even slimmer chance of you becoming a billionaire. Not every new coin can be the next Bitcoin.

Bad Strategy #3: Investing More Than You Can Afford to Lose

In stock markets and in crypto exchanges, you should not invest more than you can afford to lose. Sure, you want to buy a respectable volume of cryptocurrencies and put money in as many cryptocurrencies as possible. However, plan for the future keeping your present in mind. Do not take money out of your rainy-day fund and put it into cryptocurrency. Don't put your rent on the line in the cryptocurrency market.

There is a simple reason for it – there is no recourse in the cryptocurrency market. There is no regulator, federal banks, or corporate customer support you can get in touch with for grievance redressal. This is an emerging market and it is as risky as it is lucrative. So, weigh both sides before diving straight into the thick of this world. Carefully consider the risks and rewards along with your own personal risk tolerance before making any decisions. Remember this is not investment advice. We are only providing these topics for your consideration.

Continue to educate yourself as much as possible like you are doing now, before making any investment decision whether it is crypto currency or your nephew's new landscaping company

Bad Strategy#4: Not Diversifying Your Portfolio

If you don't diversify your financial portfolio, you are setting yourself up for a loss. For instance, do not waste time on one Altcoin and obsess over its value. Just as cost averaging takes advantage of fluctuations over time, diversification takes advantage of fluctuations over a group of different investments. Simply put, do not put all your eggs in one basket.

It makes more sense to invest in established cryptocurrencies first, and then go out on an adventure with new cryptocurrencies with a smaller amount thus diversifying your cryptocurrency portfolio.

Diversification is a necessity. If you want to build a no-nonsense cryptocurrency portfolio, start with relatively safer bets like Bitcoin and Ether. The cryptocurrency market is so volatile and these are the two safest places to park your money first. In the world of cryptocurrency, these two coins have reliable fundamentals and a long price history that can be used to predict future movements. So, if you are beginning to build an investment portfolio that includes crypto, we think starting with these two coins is a good idea. Of course, it bears repeating that you'll want to do your own research and examine these two cryptocurrencies for yourself. If, after completing your research, you decide to invest in cryptocurrency then an example of a diversified crypto portfolio might look something like, 70-75% of your portfolio to Bitcoin, the next biggest chunk of 15-20% in Ether, and the remaining 3-5% in any new Altcoins you may have faith in.

Cryptocurrency itself is going to be a highly volatile part of your overall financial portfolio. So, hedge it with safer investments like mutual funds, long-term bank deposits, real estate, gold, antiques, comic books, basically anything with value that interests you. Do not put all the cash you have in cryptocurrency. There are cryptocurrency millionaires, but there is a much larger group of people who have been burnt by it. So, tread with caution.

Bad Strategy#5: Playing with Leverage

If you are an advanced trader who has a good hold on how the value of cryptocurrency moves, invest time in tracking hourly movements, and can afford to lose some money in bad investments, leverage may help you. However, if you are new to the crypto space, you are better off avoiding leverage trading until you have mastered the basics and understand the markets. That's not a challenge, it's a cautionary warning.

A good rule of thumb would be – if you are a beginner, don't use leverage.

Leverage is a strategy where investors borrow money to invest in cryptocurrency. Basically, leverage requires you to invest money that you don't have. So, it can leave you in a pool of debt. Advanced investors use leverage to earn money by shorting and increasing their exposure.

Let's start with shorting. If you are active in stock markets, you know what shorting means. For the uninitiated, shorting is an advanced trading technique where you are betting on the market to go down. So, you borrow the cryptocurrency and sell it at a high. When the market crashes, you buy the cryptocurrency at a lower price and return to the lender. You pocket the profit from the price drop. So, if you miscalculate the direction in which the price will move, your debt can increase to dangerous levels.

Another strategy is increasing your exposure. You observe that the price of a cryptocurrency is on the rise. So, instead of buying one-hundred dollars' worth of cryptocurrency, which you have, you borrow another $900 and invest $1000. Your expectation here is that the price of the cryptocurrency will shoot up. Let's say it increases from 50 cents to 2 dollars a pop. So, your $1000 becomes $4000. You give the $900 back to the lender and have yourself a nice profit of $3000. But, that's the hope. If you increase exposure and the price tanks, you are not just out of your $100, but you are also in a $900 debt.

As you can see, using leverage can do much more than disappoint you. If you do not have a complete understanding of the cryptocurrency market, steer clear.

Bad Strategy#6: Treating it as a "Get Rich Quick" Scheme

The first thing you might be thinking is, "but what about the epic bull run Bitcoin made in 2017 a lot of investors got rich quick didn't they?" The truth is most investors did not buy in at the beginning of the bull run and even fewer investors sold at the top. Many retail investors lost money in the bull market by following Bad Strategy #1.

Here is what you need to know. The first investors in Bitcoin were not financial gurus. These were people truly interested in creating an alternative to money. They did not buy bitcoin as an investment, but as a means to buy and sell. So, they did not mine or buy bitcoin to get rich quick. But then stories of Bitcoin billionaires were sensationalized by the media. The story was you could open a Coinbase account on a Monday, invest a thousand dollars in Bitcoin on a Tuesday, make a million dollars by Wednesday, order your Lambo on a Thursday, and have it in time to take your super model date out on Saturday. It seemed like the perfect way to get rich quick.

Remember the crash of 2018. People who did not get greedy and cashed out before the 2018 crash, fared well. Those that sold before the crash knew the markets, had done their own research, did not invest emotionally, and had clearly defined entry and exit strategies. Those that sold before the crash knew that it was better to take actual profits and miss theoretical gains rather than taking actual losses. Other smart investors may have decided to hold on with diamond hands determined not to sell at a loss. In fact, in March of 2021 when the bitcoin price hit nearly $62,000 anyone who had ever invested in Bitcoin was in a profit. The point is these investors held on for the long-term knowing that year over year bitcoin always goes up. They were not investing to "Get rich Quick". They made a long-term investment they were comfortable with because they did not invest more than they could afford to lose.

Not just cryptocurrency, every investment needs due research and time; research to give you the confidence to see it through and time to create real wealth for you. So, if you are in the cryptocurrency market, investing willy-nilly to earn a quick dollar, you are treading a dangerous line. Treat it with the same respect and skepticism as you would any of your other investments. The more you know about this market, the better it will serve you.

But where should you start?

Indeed, you already have. In fact, knowing what not to do is a great place to start. Now that you have cleared your ears of all the noise, here is how you can start investing in cryptocurrency. Keep it simple. For a start, let's discuss how to buy bitcoin.

How to Buy Cryptocurrency

Usually, the "buy" step of any investment is the easiest. You have already decided what you want to buy, you are happy with the price, and all that's left is to perform the actions required to complete the transaction and purchase your crypto. As a newcomer in the world of Bitcoin, you might find it a little difficult to start buying without a little tour guide first.

You are going to find a lot of confusing information about buying bitcoin on the internet. So, it is always better to listen to an established industry name or read a good book. You are already doing it. So, you are over the first step.

At first, the process might sound a little complicated. Do not fear. We are here to guide. To get some clarity, let's start with the steps you will have to follow:

>Step#1: Create secure email account
>
>Step#2: Open a cryptoexchange account. Deposit money and buy Bitcoin
>
>Step#3: Open a crypto wallet account. Transfer your Bitcoin to wallet.
>
>Step#4: Use your new accounts to buy and sell your investment.
>
>Now that you have a map with you, it's time to start your journey. Let's start with step#1

Step 1: Create a secure email account

Every account you are going to open for trading in cryptocurrency will require you to provide an email ID. Given the sensitive nature of information that your cryptoexchange and wallets are going to hold, you have to make sure that you have an email ID that is completely secure.

The best way to start is to open a secure email account with services like Protonmail. You can add another layer of security by using 2-factor authentication such as Authy. Never forget these passwords. At this point, you might be tempted to use a password manager, but make sure you do your research on the security features of these password managers. You may use the likes of Bitwarden, but it would be preferable to go back to paper. Just ensure that you make 2-3 copies and store these notebooks with your passwords in a fire-proof safe under lock and key. The most secure place would be a safety deposit box at Fort Knox; seriously though be serious about security.

Step#2: Open a Cryptoexchange Account

In 2009, no one had ever heard of a cryptocurrency exchange. Today, there are so many that choosing one can be difficult.

While it does encourage competition and requires crypto exchanges to improve their services, it also presents a challenge to those just entering the cryptoverse. – they do not know where to start. So, let's sort that out. Here are the top ones.

Wait, you might be wondering why we don't just tell you what the best ones are, but it is not that simple.? There is no such thing as the best crypto exchange because the answer will change with your specific needs. So, it is not a question of which exchange is the best, it is a question of which exchange is the best for you.

Here are the top crypto exchanges for your consideration.

Coinbase is one of the first players in the crypto exchange space. Based out of San Francisco in the United States, the exchange boasts of over 43 million users across 100+ countries. Till 2021, the exchange has facilitated trades of more than $455billion. Coinbase is a well-known brand in the cryptocurrency circuit and provides secure offline storage, insurance coverage, and supports many popular cryptocurrencies including Bitcoins and 40 others. Given its massive scale of operations, the company itself is a multi-billion-dollar enterprise today.

The veteran exchange follows a simple sign-up process. Then, you must link your bank account. Once you enter the account, you can start placing orders right away. While there might be some variations depending on the country you belong to, the payment options at Coinbase include bank account transfers, PayPal, credit cards, and debit cards. There is a deposit and withdrawal fee that also varies depending on your mode of payment. The fee structure changes as the value of the trades go up. But, for most people the maker and taker fee will be around 0.5%. The good news is that if you want to withdraw your cryptocurrency, it's completely free!

If you pick Coinbase, you also get a customer support service. You can generate a ticket on their platform to register an issue. While most people may not need to use Coinbase customer support, when they do, well let's just say it's no 5-star service.

When it comes to security, Coinbase gets all the points. It stores 98% of its funds offline. Disconnected from the internet, the data is encrypted before being stored on USB devices along with paper backups. These are then distributed around the world and kept away in highly secure storage facilities.

Coinbase is arguably the easiest exchange to use. The fee is towards the higher side, but if you are using fiat currency and entering the cryptocurrency market, Coinbase is a great place to start.

Binance is the biggest cryptocurrency exchange on the globe. It processes a mindboggling 1.5 million transactions every second with the trades adding up to $2 billion every day!

Binance has many different country-specific versions. These are all separate from the main Binance platform. So, traders residing in Singapore, Uganda, and the United States have to trade on the Binance version for their respective country. Countries like Iran, North Korea, and others facing US sanctions are banned on Binance. Every cryptocurrency worth your time and money is listed on the Binance exchange.

When you are on Binance, you will be treated to an extensive list of features. There are also advanced derivatives products that allow traders to invest in the futures market. There are benefits like Binance Earn that earns interest like a bank deposit, Binance crypto cards that offer cashbacks, and then there are crypto loans for the users to borrow too. The range of features and other sophisticated products, offered by Biance, allows traders to use more advanced trading strategies available in the world of Bitcoin and cryptocurrency.

All the deposits on the Binance Exchange are free. There are withdrawal fees, and they depend on the cryptocurrency you are cashing out and the fiat currency you are converting it to. Deposits or withdrawals can be made using debit cards, credit cards, and bank transfers. In fact, Binance charges the lowest fee among the popular crypto exchanges. You can bring the fee down even further with discounts offered on exchanging certain cryptocurrencies and trades of higher volume.

Binance also runs its customer support round the clock and also has a ticketing system. They are known for their swift grievance redressal with the resolution time usually below 24 hours. So, it is definitely doing better than Coinbase in this department.

Binance checks all the boxes of best practices when it comes to the security of your crypto investment. These include cold storage, tiered access, multi-signature wallet, and more. However, it should be noted that the exchange was hacked of 7000 bitcoins in 2019, which came to roughly 2% of their bitcoin holdings. Like Coinbase,

98% of Binance's funds are stored away in cold storage, so they were safe. By the way, the users that lost their Bitcoin holding in the hack were reimbursed by the popular SAFU fund of Binance.

Binance is certainly a favorite among advanced traders. It is especially preferred by traders who have their eyes on Altcoins.

The next on our list, of the cryptoexchanges that you should know about, is Kraken. Founded in 2011, this exchange predates pioneers like Coinbase. It was founded by a MtGox trader who witnessed the biggest Bitcoin hacks in history. He was convinced that he could do a much better job than the now defunct MtGox at running an exchange.

Headquartered in San Francisco, Kraken exchange has millions of users and is valued over 4 billion. This valuation easily makes it among the top 3 cryptoexchanges alongside Coinbase and Binance. The exchange is the choice of a lot of institutional investors, who bring in hundreds of millions of dollars.

Kraken is an old competitor, so it has been testing its security protocol for a long time. They keep 95% of their cryptocurrency offline and it is distributed worldwide. Kraken also takes serious security measures for server security with 24x7 armed personnel on-site, CCTV monitoring, and more. So, hackers don't just need coding power, but gun power to get a piece of their data. Kraken supports trading for all the major cryptocurrencies. However, you won't find obscure Altcoins here.

While Kraken is available across the continents, there are a few countries it does not serve. The residents of Japan, Cuba, Afghanistan, Iraq, Iran, North Korea, and Tajikistan cannot trade on Kraken. It is also not available in New York and Washington State.

For deposits, Kraken is either free or charges a small flat fee. The maker and taker fee for most people is in the bracket of 0.16 to 0.26%, which is almost half of Coinbase.

Verification process on Kraken usually takes longer than other exchanges. To deposit fiat currency, you have to upload a valid ID, proof of residence, valid Social Security Number, and face photographs. Once verified, then you can deposit the currency and start trading. As you start trading, you will notice the long list of features offered by Kraken.

Customer support at Kraken includes 24X7 live chat support and is certainly one of the best among the competition. You can speak directly with a human customer support agent in a matter of seconds., They will answer your questions so you can get back to trading. Start out with any of these three exchanges. The choice depends on the country you are from, the fees you are ready to pay, and the cryptocurrencies you want to trade in.

Step#3: Open a Crypto Wallet Account

Now you have bought the cryptocurrency, it's time to store it. You can store it online or in an offline vault. This is where a crypto wallet comes in!

A cryptowallet is essentially a tool for you to engage with a blockchain network. Here is the simplest possible transaction for you.

Peter is transferring one bitcoin to Sarah. The wallet generates a private key and a public key. These have to be generated in pairs. The public key now generates a bitcoin address.

Sarah gives Peter the address, and Peter transfers 1 Bitcoin from his account to Sarah's account. Keep in mind that the number of bitcoins in this blockchain remained the same, they were only transferred from one address to another. No new bitcoin was created.

Sharing the bitcoin address is safe. However, Sarah should never share the private key or secret phrase with anyone.

These are the bare fundamentals. Let's take it up a notch to come closer to what's available in the real world. You can choose between hot wallets and cold wallets.

A crypto wallet is about 3 pieces of information – private keys, public keys, and bitcoin addresses. Of the 3 pieces of information, the private key is the most sensitive, and you should never reveal it to anyone. The individual who has access to her private key can transfer her bitcoins to any address. You can use the private key to access her wallet from any device. This private key can also be used to generate new public key and blockchain address. So, you need to have a secure backup of their private keys.

Modern wallets may use seed phrases that generate private keys. So, you need to take the backup of the seed phrase, which can then be used to generate multiple private keys.

A hot wallet is a virtual entity. When you buy bitcoins from an exchange and deposit it in the exchange, you are depositing the bitcoins in a hot wallet. Unsurprisingly, these are the most convenient for traders who need to use the wallet frequently. The software wallets can further be divided into three types – web, desktop, and mobile. A web wallet is exclusively available online. It does not even require you to download or install a software. You use a browser interface to use the wallet. A desktop wallet requires you to download a software and install it on your device. When it comes to security, these rank above web wallets. Mobile wallets are the same as a desktop wallet but designed for mobile devices.

Then, there are cold wallets which are not connected to the internet. The physical wallets store the private keys offline. Automatically, they are safer than hot wallets. Popularly known as "cold storage", these wallets are the first choice of long-term and big investors. Cold wallets include hardware wallets and paper wallets. Hardware wallets are physical devices that use random number generators for public and private keys that are stored in the device. They do not need any online connection to generate or store them. While obsolete, let's discuss the paper wallets too while we are at it. A paper wallet is essentially a piece of paper that contains a blockchain address and its private key in QR code format. So, you can scan the QR code and then send or receive funds on it. Paper wallets are on the verge of going out of use because they cannot send a fraction of funds. While its secure, the possibility of cleaning out your account with one transaction is high.

The important thing to remember is to create secure passwords for any wallet you may choose and take regular backups of the seed phrases, private keys, and wallet data files. You want to keep the account secure, but it is crucial that you yourself do not lose access to your cryptocurrency vault.

From a paper to hardware to online services, there are a lot of bitcoin wallets to choose from. Of course, each wallet type offers its own benefits, and falls at a different spot in the "safety" spectrum.

Once you have created a Bitcoin wallet, you can start trading on exchanges, but there is another way. You can sell bitcoins directly to brokers. They do charge a higher fee. However, given the intimidating interface of exchanges, a broker offers a quick transaction. This is suitable for beginners who are just looking to test waters in the Bitcoin market.

If it is your first purchase, using a reputed broker might be less intimidating than a busy exchange. All you have to do is to get a Bitcoin wallet, get hold of your Bitcoin address, and start buying!

Congratulations, now you know how to become a Bitcoin owner.

Chapter 5
DeFi Craze, 2020 and Beyond!

You have covered everything there is to know about the fundamentals of cryptocurrency. You know the technology, you know the product, and you know how to own it. Now, it's time to become a savvy cryptocurrency investor, trader, and owner – whatever you want to be. You are going to own the currency of the future. The world is moving towards a DeFi future. That future is inevitable.

So, what is DeFi?

DeFi is short for Decentralized Finance. But, in essence, DeFi refers to the use of cryptocurrency or blockchain technology to disrupt the usual financial models run by intermediaries. Bain Capital Venture's partner states that people like DeFi because "they have a libertarian streak".

Rewind back to the chapter on Blockchain technology where we spoke about the applications of blockchain. Bitcoin is one of the applications of blockchain. While Ethereum uses blockchain technology to create smart contracts for various applications.

The one application of DeFi – cryptocurrency – has already rattled the world. The idea behind cryptocurrency was also to take money out of the clutches of the government. Fiat currencies are heavily influenced by government policy. Wall Street can halt trading and get bailed out if the market does not behave well. Centralized banks can make bad decisions, push economies into recession, and still get stimulus packages from Federal reserves to bounce back. DeFi is the ultimate financial equalizer that takes the power out of the hands of a few and places it in the hands of the many. DeFi is controlled by vast computer networks, investors, traders, and miners. Its movement lies completely outside the jurisdiction of governments or any other central authority. Along with privacy and anonymity DeFi promises newfound levels of freedom.

DeFi is a giant step towards this freedom. It promises an ecosystem where the existing and familiar financial instruments can be used by people without working under the shadow of a central authority. Managing Partners of the $100 million crypto fund, Dragonfly Capital, puts it succinctly, "The goal of DeFi is to reconstruct the banking system for the whole world in this open, permissionless way. You only get that shot every 50 years."

There are many examples around the world that highlight the need to replace current financial institutions with decentralized finance. But none illustrate that need more tragically than the failed state of Venezuela.

Venezuela is a resource-rich country. With plentiful oil reserves, it had become one of the richest countries in South America. Despite its natural wealth, a steep drop in international crude oil prices and poor governance lead to financial ruin.

Incredibly, the country went from being among the wealthiest to becoming one the poorest countries in the region. At its worst, the annual inflation rate in Venezuela was 350,000% in 2019. While the drop in crude oil prices was a setback, it was the government and the federal banks that created the calamity.

This failure at the very top makes the case for DeFi even stronger. With DeFi, people no longer have to worry about their life savings being destroyed by the rather subjective factor of political will. **With DeFi the national Flag flying over your head becomes irrelevant to your financial life.** People will be empowered to conduct business from anywhere in the world. So, they can move funds, invest in different asset classes, and enjoy a greater control over their own financial future.

While the Venezuelan economy offers a compelling case study, a more recent upheaval in the financial markets has again shed light on the necessity of going the DeFi route. If there is a time for DeFi to make a grand entrance, the GameStop fiasco was it.

If you are not aware, here is a little background for you – GameStop is a chain of retail stores that are a common fixture across malls in the United States. For a long time, the company's fundamentals had been poor. Why would a computer-savvy gamer visit a physical store instead of downloading the game online? Their sales had been dropping consistently, and in 2019 they touched a new low of $1.8billion. With no rebound plan, the company was doomed. Undoubtedly, it was a bad investment. Big Wall Street hedge funds like Melvin Securities and Citadel Securities thought likewise. In fact, Citadel Securities is the biggest customer of Robinhood. Both these hedge funds held millions of Gamestop shares. Their strategy was to short the Gamestop shares, push the company to its end, and get out with a profit of millions of dollars.

But a subreddit had other plans. A small group of investors contributing to the

Reddit thread called WallStreetBets saw the plan of the Wall Street elite. They wanted to put the power back in the hands of the unsuspecting small retail investors of GameStop and give the black suits a taste of their own medicine. And boy, they did. The market capitalization of GameStop went from $650 million in the latter half of 2020 to $28billion on January 28.

But what happened next hammered home the need for a DeFi system. Robinhood stepped in. The platform that ironically exists to "democratize finance for all", prevented its retail customers from buying and selling the GameStop stock. Reportedly, this was done under the pressure from the big hedge funds. Other similar platforms like E-Trade and Ameritrade mirrored the move. But Robinhood took the heat from the investors. A Twitter storm ensued that resonated the need for a system without such censorship.

Cryptoexhchange Gemini's President said, "The pandemic made people appreciate #Bitcoin as an inflation hedge. The deplatforming of Wall Street Bets is making everyone appreciate it's censorship resistance." *(honestly this event is what caused us to want to complete this book so quickly, Defi is my personal 1776, my 4th of July, my Declaration of Independence ~Shawn)*

Blockchain.com's founder also chimed in, "A shot across the bow for institutional investors everywhere, there's incredible power in decentralized groups of individuals and the future of finance will be built less like Wall Street and more like the internet: by a decentralized group of individuals. My thoughts and prayers are with the many institutions that will learn this lesson the hard way."

Many other financial experts and guru's joined Blockchain.com and Cryptoexchange in condemning the heavy-handed censorship that was on display during the GameStop incident.

Unlike Wall Street a cryptoexchange makes it impossible for such events to occur in the first place. Even if the promoter of a cryptoexchange is influenced, they have no control over the flow of its funds which is ensured by its distributed nature and democratic functioning.

DeFi is of the people, for the people, and by the people. That's by immutable design.

Chapter 6
Way Forward

Mass adoption has already begun. Most CEO and CFO's of major corporations would be fired today if they could not show BitCoin was part of their companies holdings. Elon Musk Richest man in the World now openly supports Crypto. He said in retrospect it was inevitable.

The interest in cryptocurrency and DeFi has exponentially increased and does not seem to be a flash in the pan anymore. Mass adoption may still be a little in the future, but the stage has already been set. The latest push to a cryptocurrency market came from the most unlikely place – the pandemic. With the growth of all types of digital technologies in finance, cryptocurrency also boomed.

It is undeniable that cryptocurrency did not make the best first impressions. It was seen as an inaccessible method of money movement used in the dark web for illegal activities. But Bitcoin from its inception till date has been clear on its motive – a decentralized system of finance.

Its volatility was discouraging to people that looked at it as an asset class. But, given the unprecedented returns that Bitcoin has earned its investors and a growing demand for DeFi solutions, investments in cryptocurrencies are on the rise.

An industry report by BeInCrypto reports that the adoption of cryptocurrency wallets has tripled since 2017. On the ground too, you can see a change in attitude towards cryptocurrency. Small vendors have started accepting bitcoin as a mode of payment. As this catches up, which it already is, wholesalers will also move to bitcoin payments from retailers. As the back end starts running on cryptocurrency. The payments will be buffered from the volatility the same way businesses account for international payments in foreign currencies. With B2B and B2C business accepting bitcoin, rents, mortgages, and even salaries will convert to cryptocurrency. As this adoption continues, cryptocurrency may even get detached from fiat currency values and become an independent financial system.

While adoption among the general public may still take years, the adoption is already apparent among the corporates. Until now, Google had kept a conspicuous distance from the world of cryptocurrency. However, with a surge in demand for cryptocurrencies among people, new business opportunities are cropping up. Customers are actively looking for reliable names to make transactions. At the same time, cryptocurrency companies are making an effort to offer their services in a more user-friendly and accessible fashion. Google has recognized the potential of this opportunity and is now offering its hugely successful Google Pay payment method available to these crypto firms. A prominent example comes from Coinbase. Google allowed the Coinbase card to be added to Google Play as a method of paying for products and services.

Elon Musk, the on and off richest man on Earth shared his views on cryptocurrency calling it, "Future Currency of Earth". Elon Musk has not been shy about his fondness of cryptocurrency. His tweet about Dogecoin drove the prices of the cryptocurrency 300%. Then came February 8, when Tesla went ahead and bought a mind-boggling $1.5billion in Bitcoin. In fact, the company is planning to include Bitcoin as a method of payment for their products. As the news came out, Bitcoin went on an upward trajectory reaching a never-seen-before high of $58,000.

With the recent pandemic eating away economies, commodities and cryptocurrencies have emerged as promising hedges to counter inflation. Corporations are now adding cryptocurrency as an asset class in their books. In December 2020 MicroStrategy Incorporated, a NASDAQ listed company announced that they invested over $1 billion in Bitcoin purchases in 2020. They hold Bitcoin in their balance sheet. Since the adoption, their share prices increased 4 times. In fact, it has outperformed Bitcoin itself. The CEO of the company explained the unconventional move by the company, saying,

"This investment reflects our belief that Bitcoin, as the world's most widely-adopted cryptocurrency, is a dependable store of value and an attractive investment asset with more long-term appreciation potential than holding cash. Since its inception over a decade ago, Bitcoin has emerged as a significant addition to the global financial system, with characteristics that are useful to both individuals and institutions. MicroStrategy has recognized Bitcoin as a legitimate investment asset that can be superior to cash and accordingly has made Bitcoin the principal holding in its treasury reserve strategy."

He further added that it was not a short-term hedge, but a long-term investment in recognition of the future of the global financial markets.

"Our belief is that Bitcoin is the first effective digital monetary network, and it's going to grow over time. We're early adopters, the early Bitcoin holders or adopters. It's the solution to every company's problem and every individual investor's problem. And so as more and more corporations adopt the Bitcoin's standard and they use it as a store of value, as more investors and mutual funds and hedge funds use it as a store of value, as more individuals use it as a store of value, the overall amount of monetary energy, the total amount of capital flowing into the network is just going to increase in time. And because there's a fixed amount of Bitcoin, that just means the price is going to go up."

Apart from MicroStrategy, Google, and Tesla, there are many other CEOs who see the potential of Bitcoin to change the financial world as we know it. One of the most notable among them is Jack Dorsey, who serves as the CEO of Twitter and Square. In fact, Dorsey's Twitter bio reads and we quote – "#bitcoin". Twitter does not formally hold Bitcoin in its books, but its CFO has been quoted mulling the idea of holding and using Bitcoin. The other company, Square, has gone much bolder with Bitcoin. As much as 5% of the company's shares are invested in Bitcoin. No prizes for guessing that it is only a matter of time that we will see Twitter formally joining the Bitcoin bandwagon.

CEOs, CFOs, financial experts, and commonfolk are slowly warming up to Bitcoin and blockchain. They are recognizing it as a new means of transacting and investing. But, still, there are many obstacles that stand between cryptocurrency and mass adoption. These include the inherent complexity of the cryptocurrency concept, its bad past reputation, too many crypto assets, high volatility, and the huge global digital divide. Of course, these are real problems that need to be addressed. Rome was not built in a day and neither will be a DeFi crypto world.

And it is definitely worth the wait.

Chapter 7
Can I Make a Career Out of Crypto?

Let's put an end to any and all speculation on this subject – anyone and absolutely anyone can make a career out of crypto. No exceptions.

You need to have a willingness to learn, the patience to research, and a stomach that can take the short-term extreme market swings. There are many ways in which you can start a career in the cryptocurrency space. After all, the job opportunities have exploded in this industry with the job market growing 20 times between 2011 and 2017.

Of course, this is a high-growth industry, but is it a high-growth industry that you want to be a part of? Here are a few reasons why people pursue a career in this industry.

The no.1 reason is the highly resilient nature of the industry to natural disasters like the COVID19 pandemic. The entire industry works online. So, any disruption in the flow of labor or resources does not affect the industry or the income of the people working in it.

The second reason is the ability to work from any part of the world as long as you have an active internet connection. It also promises high returns to early adopters. Think of it like holding a Google stock before it became the king of online search engines.

Since people are learning on the job, there is no defined skill set for applicants to get a job. And that's a compelling third reason. You do not need any formal education or have to fit a certain mold; it is an open house. Anyone with the ability to contribute to the industry can join in. There are no defined eligibility requirements, yet. So, it is rather easy to climb up the corporate ladder in cryptocurrency companies. The journey to the top is a short one.

Finally, the cryptocurrency space is evolving. So, the job you get is fast-paced and comes with limitless potential to learn. This is not a 9 to 5 mind-numbing job. It will present new challenges every single day that require innovative and fresh solutions.

So, now you understand the reasons people want to be employed in the industry, let's find out how you can get in.

Trading in Crypto is the first obvious career opportunity that pops into mind. And it can be a start of a flourishing career. Right now, you have the deck stacked in your favor. Cryptocurrency, in particular, and blockchain technology, in general is still in its early phases right now. As people and businesses find more applications for them, their usage is going to grow. With the growing use, the value of your portfolio will grow too.

At this moment, cryptocurrency is in its nascent stage. You have the opportunity to get in on the ground floor of this emerging opportunity. You can certainly make money with cryptocurrency trading. With a very small percentage of people trading on cryptoexchanges, the income potential is high.

You can do much more with cryptocurrencies than trade. We are not just talking about becoming a Bitcoin millionaire here. Try to widen your perspective, and you will realize the massive opportunity that is staring back at you. Think of cryptocurrency as value investing. You are investing in a decentralized financial future. Do your research and find cryptocurrencies where you see potential and invest in them like you would in different stocks. There will be hits and misses, but with a good mix of investments, you will see your portfolio grow.

You can start a career working for one of the companies working in the cryptocurrency space. Most of the core jobs will understandably revolve around software development. These include full stack engineers, dev ops engineer, blockchain engineer, and so on. Other job opportunities belong to the disciplines of marketing, content management, research, customer service, human resources, and law. Interestingly enough, most of these jobs pay more than average as opposed to their counterparts in other industries.

To find a job in the cryptocurrency industry, the drill is the same – scrolling through job boards like CryptoJobsList, CryptoJobs, CryptocurrencyJobs, and more. Today, there are dedicated job boards that list jobs exclusively in this space. Alternatively, you can visit the company websites dealing in cryptocurrency and apply directly. These companies include cryptoexchanges like Coinbase, Binance, and Kraken, cryptowallets like Ledger and Atomic, content creators for the industry like blogs, YouTube channels, and more. You can also become part of many crypto projects that are in their infancy and start from scratch.

Cryptocurrency is a small space. So, go out to seminars, join discussion forums, and other social platforms that revolve around cryptocurrency. It is highly likely that you will find yourself a job offer by networking with the right people.

Even more important is ensuring that you are working with the right people and a legitimate crypto project. If at any point you feel that you are in the wrong crowd, don't hesitate to exit. The breakneck speed of the industry guarantees that you will find another job.

From the insane amount of news that comes out of the cryptoworld, it is easy to assume that you have missed the bus to any substantial profit from the industry. However, that is far from the truth. Whether you are an active trader, a long-term investor, or someone looking for a job in the industry, it's a great time to join this fledgling industry.

Start your crypto journey, you have all the tools in your armor. All that is left to do is deploy!

Are you ready? Get Set...

www.ingramcontent.com/pod-product-compliance
Lightning Source LLC
Chambersburg PA
CBHW071423210526
45465CB00001B/504